AF582954

p.s. Fortuna

Praises & Supplications

For the Goddess

by E. Sylvia

This book is dedicated to all lost and found animal friends and to those who lovingly care for them.

Table of Contents

Preface

I began sharing my interest in the Goddess Fortuna with online communities in 2009. One of the first things I noticed was a common belief that She "didn't have any stories", that She "represented a concept" and not a "real" flesh-and-blood sort of Goddess. She wasn't Diana, whom everyone has heard of, nor was She Lakshmi the Hindu wealth Goddess, or even Arachne who, at least, had a memorable fable. Hardly anyone seemed to know about the Goddess Fortuna, especially me!

Fortunately, Thalia Took's wonderful "Obscure Goddess Online Directory" was ranking high in the search engines at the time, and hopefully still is. Despite complaints from my peers her amateur research lacked the footnotes of academia, the threads in Thalia's fabric of Fortuna's tapestry held strong. Numerous anonymous Wikipedians, and resources like A.S. Klein's online translation of Ovid's *Fasti*, helped me verify the stories, characters, and flesh out the "real" Goddess Fortuna. Who did Fortuna represent, how was She real, and what did She believe in?

I discovered one basic fact: The Goddess Fortuna is reliable and discrete; a divine princess who is here to stay, and not to show off. Despite changes in religious and spiritual expression since the days of the Roman Empire, She hasn't changed much, and She never really left us. She graced the Rota Fortunae of the Middle Ages, and appeared as a winged angel in one of the first known tarot's Wheel of Fortune. She inspired a 20th century television show, numerous spin-offs and games. Her statues show up in casinos; Her name graces an elaborate Las Vegas swimming pool.

It's not that the Goddess Fortuna doesn't have stories. She does. Aesop tells several stories of Fortuna (as the Greek Tyche) which tell how little She has changed, and how little we have changed at the same time. A common thread is wise guidance offered to humans, humans who are at risk of either ignoring Fortuna's advice or taking Her for granted, and humans who choose to blame Fortuna for things which are our own fault. It's hardly a surprise to hear "Fortuna has no stories", when we are in the habit of paying attention to flashier or more dramatic Goddesses.

Very pretty contemporary statuettes of the Goddess Fortuna portray Her blindfolded; carelessly spilling coins from an overturned cornucopia. I once purchased a lovely statuette in this iconic style, which I eventually placed on a high shelf amidst other wonderful objects. I can look up and marvel as I imagine those coins dropping down to me from above. In real life, Fortuna has not actually opened doors to tons of money, despite my diligent efforts to improve my career over the years. Clearly, to me at least, Fortuna does not understand money the same way that I do.

Eventually a second style of Fortuna statuette appeared for sale; a small gypsum replica, far less beautiful than the first. Sexy, low-cut blouses, Barbie-perfect thighs peeking through slit skirts and gaudy jewelry are nowhere to be seen in this humble statue. Her face does not show classic symmetry, and her details are a little sketchy. True to form, though, the replica shows a serious Goddess in a traditional pose, dressed very modestly in Roman garb, with a securely held, upright cornucopia full of precious and valuable produce to provide for Her people. A deity.

I've kept this little, traditional replica in a small wall niche for several years, at a height where the activity of my household takes place. Here is where incense is close at hand, candles are lit, the intentions are set and divination takes place. One day, as I lit a candle, my hand brushed against Her, and She toppled down into my kitchen sink, breaking off her cornucopia. I felt Her sadness at all the destruction of Her statues over the centuries, and glued the piece back on with care. I'm comfortable with this humble, repaired replica, and greatly appreciate both statues.

Contemporary spiritual and magical correspondences for the Goddess Fortuna focus strongly on portraying Her as a bringer of wealth prosperity, rather than in Her traditional role as a bringer of "good fortune" of an abundant fruit harvest, and all the other types of luck for which the ancients named Her. In a search for Her symbols, I discovered there is not a lot of agreement for what actually belongs to the Goddess Fortuna. Different aspects of this Goddess have inspired many different and wonderful ideas.

My favorites from Her contemporary symbolism include:

Color: gold, yellow; colors of success, the sun, and the harvest.

Symbols: The cornucopia, filled with fruit.

Amulet: The Tarot major arcana Wheel of Fortune card.

Mineral: Aventurine, which comes in a wide range of colors.

Plant or scent: Bergamot fruit, an ingredient that gives Earl Grey tea its delicious distinction.

Day: Any day, or every day, when it's convenient. For example: Sunday for Good Fortune, Monday as Juno's daughter, Tuesday for goal setting, Wednesday for divination, Thursday as Jupiter's daughter, Friday as Fortuna-Venus, Saturday for harvest from the earth.

Compass Directions: East, for the rising sun and the spring season; a beginning point for the turning of Her wheel. South, for the noonday sun and the summer season; the fruit harvest.

Numerous ancient epithets of the Goddess appear on websites like Wikipedia. They might look something like this:

Primigenia, Virilis, Virginalis, Venus, Fors, Redux, Muliebris, Equestris, Huiusque Diei, Privita, Publica…

How to choose? My advice, from personal experience, is don't worry about the epithets. Aspects were important, in ancient times, for members of a vast Roman republic who all worshipped Fortuna. These ancients may have felt a need to distinguish a prayer for good luck with their newborn from good luck in the battlefield. If you enjoy studying aspects, go for it. However; I believe contemporary practice doesn't need to make such distinctions. It's enough, for this Goddess, that we recognize, respect, and remember Her on a regular basis as one female deity.

If Her correspondences and symbols don't resonate with you, don't worry about that either. Remember those Aesop fables I mentioned earlier? Aesop and the Orphic hymns are in perfect agreement as to what the Goddess Fortuna prefers: the scent of Frankincense. In my opinion, this is the most powerful way to reach the Goddess Fortuna; either through anointing a candle with (diluted) frankincense essential oil or burning incense (pure, stick or cone). I like to do this daily, or at least once a week, to become more and more actively present in a caring, spiritual energy.

Fortunately, the worst ancient ways of worship are obsolete these days. However; it's nice to find appropriate, acceptable symbols and correspondences from the distant past. Here are a few:

Offering: frankincense, according to Greek authors from antiquity.

Colors: purple, red, yellow; colors of harvest fruits, as shown in the colors of Her gowns on ancient painted frescos.

Amulet: Roman coins and intaglio jewelry were engraved with deities. Images may show Fortuna with a cornucopia, and coins often spell out Her name and/or epithet as well.

Symbols: Rudder or globe; symbolizing navigation by ship and world travel.

Minerals: Romans intaglios appear to be mostly made of carnelian gemstone, and set in gold or silver. Larger statues were usually of marble or bronze, and statuettes might also be made of bronze.

Plant or scent: all harvest fruits, e.g. grapes, apples, occasional exotic fruits like pineapple

Consort: Bonus Eventus, a masculine harvest deity, as seen on ancient Roman coins.

Day: Holidays were often established on the date of a regional temple dedication. Temples to the Goddess Fortuna were sometimes built to commemorate events that were considered unexpectedly and/or importantly lucky.

Animal: Horse; the steed of Rome's *Ordo Equestris*

I like to keep a permanent altar to the Goddess Fortuna, with a statue that is in an arched niche that a designer kindly devised in the wall between my kitchen and living room. If you don't have a niche, a large, deep shadow box hung on the wall might work in a similar way. A shelf might also work, although I like the idea of the Goddess having Her own "roof" over Her head. Items on my altar include a small Goddess statue, a tea-size candle holder, and crystals.

I also have several of Her ancient coins tucked away (the common types which may be acquired inexpensively at online auction) for historic and spiritual significance rather than as offerings. Because it was not Fortuna, but Her mother the Goddess Juno, who was affiliated with the Roman treasury in the aspect of Juno Moneta (from whom the word *money* is derived), it is my experience that offering these coins to Fortuna is practically meaningless on a practical or financial level. Besides, ancient coins can't be used in the contemporary marketplace.

Instead, I like the idea of using everyday coinage for divination purposes. Fortuna was a genius at oracular advice, with the second most popular oracle to the one at Delphi. Not to mention Her symbolic role in the tarot major arcana, as the Wheel of Fortune. Traditionally, tossing a coin to see whether it lands "heads" or "tails" have been used to answer simple "yes" or "no" questions or even to make a decision. It might be interesting to try using different types of coins, or coins with significant years on them, and see when the answer comes true or the decision is made wisely.

In addition to expanding my creativity and knowledge, and practicing simple divination, since welcoming the Goddess Fortuna regularly into my spiritual practice I've found it's become much easier for me to notice precious moments of unusual luck in real life; from finding a convenient parking space for winter holiday shopping, to exuberantly selecting the best produce at the farmers market, to becoming more compassionate for my friends and family. I don't have to be a mega-billion-heiress to recognize good fortune. Sometimes simple pleasures are truly priceless.

E. Sylvia April 2017

TO FORTUNA

The Fumigation from Frankincense

Orphic Hymn 71

Introduction

Her Story

There are quite a few ancient holidays of the Roman Goddess Fortuna throughout the year with Her stories, legends and history that I have researched from my location in the USA, where the word "Rome" brings images of a romantic, ancient city of the Vatican. We imagine, perhaps, something a little like Las Vegas and a little like Paris, with maybe a touch of New York City. This is the salient point: we envision a city, not an empire. However, in its greatest, largest extent, as an empire Rome was comparable in size to the United States of America.

Rome began as a fairly small Italian community in the hills, and grew to include parts of Europe, the United Kingdom, the Middle East and Africa; quite impressive indeed. After the "fall" of Rome, the culture moved eastward to Constantinople, which converted from Paganism to Christianity over a period of centuries.

To Roman citizens, the most important deities were Jupiter, Juno and Minerva, who represented the family structure in temples in and near public spaces frequented by the community. These deities are believed to be inherited, by the Roman religion, from Hellenic Olympians Zeus, Hera and Athena of Pagan Greek religion. The Goddess Fortuna, believed to be the Roman version of an Oceanid named Tyche, was reputed to have removed her wings and sandals to stay in Rome. Rome also gave Her a new lineage: the firstborn, or first-bearing, daughter of Jupiter and Juno.

Sporting a mural (castellated) crown, both Fortuna and Tyche represented good luck in matters of security and safety. Fortuna's Roman Temples were designed and built, as vowed by successful military leaders, emperors, kings and, in at least one situation, by a mother. Fortuna was known as a Goddess who recognized all Her people; from the emperor and military leaders to non-citizens and slaves. Men, women and babies all had a place at Fortuna's' celebrations, and Tyche's image would represent the fortifications and the personification of the "New Rome", Constantinople.

According to Howard Rollin Patch, in *The Tradition of the Goddess Fortuna, in Roman Literature and in the Transitional Period,* Fortuna had *at least 28 different functions and cognomina* (aspects). Some have been found in altar inscriptions, and some were represented in official temples and holidays within the city of Rome and other important cities within the enormous Empire. The next part of the introduction to this book shares some history of Fortuna's holidays (in the city of Rome unless noted otherwise) and, if known, how they were celebrated in ancient times.

Historic holidays are not necessarily appropriate, affordable or ethical to duplicate in contemporary worship. If an ancient holiday ritual appeals to you, it's a good idea to write down an adaptation that is appropriate for your situation, your schedule and your location. A ritual bath, a cup of tea or coffee, or vase filled with water might substitute for a river; a coin, dice or a set of runes for oracle lots, and so forth. According to ancient sources, Fortuna (as the Greek Tyche) appreciated offerings of frankincense, and kind acts of mercy for the unfortunate.

I hope you will enjoy this brief time travel into Rome's past, to look at the Goddess Fortuna from a new-old point of view. In researching these holidays, I discovered many things to relate to as a human being in the new millennium, representing timeless human needs, desires, and aspirations. Perhaps you will, as have I, become more intuitively aware of the enormous living energy, in time and space, of the ancient and intensely competitive Empire of dedicated and vibrant Pagan Romans, in contrast to an elegant, if antiquated, city of religion and romance.

Around the Year
with the Goddess Fortuna

INVENIT TAMEN INTER HAS UTRASQUE SENTENTIAS MEDIUM SIBI IPSA MORTALITAS NUMEN QUO MINUS ETIAM PLANA DE DEO CONIECTATIO ESSET TOTO QUIPPE MUNDO ET OMNIBUS LOCIS OMNIBUSQUE HORIS OMNIUM VOCIBUS FORTUNA SOLA INVOCATUR AC NOMINATUR UNA ACCUSATUR REA UNA AGITUR UNA COGITATUR SOLA LAUDATUR SOLA ARGUITUR ET CUM CONVICIIS COLITUR VOLUBILIS

QUE A PLERISQUE VERO ET CAECA EXISTIMATA VAGA INCONSTANS INCERTA VARIA INDIGNORUMQUE FAUTRIX HUIC OMNIA EXPENSA HUIC FERUNTUR ACCEPTA ET IN TOTA RATIONE MORTALIUM SOLA UTRAMQUE PAGINAM FACIT ADEOQUE OBNOXIAE SUMUS SORTIS UT PRORSUS IPSA PRO DEO SIT QUA DEUS PROBATUR INCERTUS

Among these discordant opinions mankind have discovered for themselves a kind of intermediate deity, by which our skepticism concerning the divine is still increased.

For all over the world, in all places, and at all times, Fortuna is the only Goddess whom everyone invokes; She alone is spoken of, She alone is accused and is supposed to be guilty; She alone is in our thoughts, is praised and blamed and loaded with reproaches; wavering as She is, conceived by the generality of mankind to be blind, wandering, inconstant, uncertain, variable, and often favouring the unworthy.

To Her are referred all our losses and all our gains, and in casting up the accounts of mortals She alone balances the two pages of our sheet. We are so much in the power of chance, that Fortuna Herself is considered as divine and the existence of the divine becomes doubtful.

Regarding God Chapter 5 (Book 7) from *The Natural History*
by Gaius Plinius Secundus (Pliny the Elder)
adapted from the Latin translation by John Bostock and H. T. Riley
(1872)

January

January 1, Day of the Goddess Fortuna, was established by the Emperor Trajan in the second century of the Common Era in a Temple dedicated on this day with offerings to Fortuna in all Her aspects. The Emperor Trajan, originally from Spain, greatly expanded the Roman Empire; inscriptions to Fortuna Salutaris and Balnearis (aspects of health and the bath) have reportedly been found in the baths of Roman forts as far from Rome as the United Kingdom. Temple dedications to medicinal healing deities Aesculapius and Vediovis were also held on January 1st.

February through March

Holidays for the Goddess Fortuna do not occur during these months., and resume in April.

April

April 1, Day of Fortuna Virilis, coordinated with Veneralia and Day of Venus Verticordia. Her Temple was dedicated in 114 BCE. The statue of Fortuna Virilis was displayed with gold necklaces; perhaps offerings made throughout the year. According to Ovid's Fasti, this holiday was celebrated by removing the gold necklaces from the statue and then bathing the statue. The statue was then consecrated with offerings of fresh flowers, roses, poppies, milk, and honey in the comb. Women bathed under a myrtle tree, so that their husbands would always love them.

April 5, Day of Fortuna Publica, according to Ovid's Fasti, was named for a temple dedicated on the Quirinal hill on this calendar date. This fact is stated briefly in very pretty and conservative poetry, which describes the dawn of a new day. This style of writing may poetically imply that the holiday was celebrated quietly and conservatively with pretty or fragrant botanical offerings, in contrast with the passage which precedes it; a wild, lengthy description of lurid details regarding a festival to Cybele that was celebrated from April 4th through 10th.

April 11, Oracle of Fortuna Patet at the fabulous Temple Complex of Fortuna Primigenia in the ancient city of Praeneste (Palestrina), Italy. One of the most famous oracles of the ancient world, comparable to the oracle at Delphi; divination for mothers and their newborn babies took place continuously for hundreds of years. It's easy to imagine an energetic pilgrimage to the complex, and up the grand stairway to the third floor temple of Fortuna Primigenia, where oak lots were selected from an olive wood box by a young boy under the divine guidance of the Goddess.

May

May 11, Tyche-Fortuna Anthousa was the tutelary Goddess of Constantinople on the city's dedication day in 330 CE. Coinage linking the Goddess Tyche to Dea Roma was distributed as Constantinople's currency, according to Lars Ramskold and Noel Lenski in *Constantinople's Dedication Medallions and the Maintenance of Civic Traditions*, who state this evidence of Constantine's tie with Rome as a desire for acceptance of Hellenic Paganism. This, the new capital of the Roman Empire (Byzantium), was established before the fall of the city of Rome to invading forces.

May 25, Day of Fortuna Publica Populi Romani (Fortuna of Rome's Public Population) was for a Temple dedicated in 194 BCE, with perhaps similarly unremarkable celebrations as the Fortuna Publica holiday in April. The dedication appeared to honor victory and overseas expansion of the Roman Empire. In the Fasti, Ovid writes poetically about the power of the Roman Empire, the seas as governed by the wife of Neptune, and the eagle as a symbol of the deity Jove; yet instead of describing festivities, he merely states the holiday will be remembered.

June

June 10, Day of Fortuna Virilis, was the second day of a week-long Vestalia, the most important festival to the Goddess Vesta. Ovid writes cryptically and briefly in this, the last known recorded month of the Fasti, about violets, mules, millstones grinding grain, and sailors looking for the dolphin at night. The Dolphin may subtly refer to informal extramarital consummation rituals of Fortuna Virilis in the public baths, or observance of the Delphinus constellation's eastern rising in June. Ovid does not give details about how the holiday was celebrated.

June 11, Day Fortuna Virginalis, coincided with the Vestalia and the Matralia of the Mater Matuta, when the inner sanctuary of the Temple to Vesta was open to the public. As offerings for the Goddess for blessings on their children, mothers would bake traditional cakes in earthenware pots. Wealthy families, who arranged marriages for their daughters, protected the husbands from becoming attracted to servant women by forbidding female servants from entering Her sacred temple during the Matralia.

June 24, Day of Fors Fortuna (summer solstice) was a 6th century BCE temple dedication to Fors Fortuna and a joyful celebration of transformation from powerlessness to wealth and power. Servius Tullius, a servant rumored to be beloved of the Goddess Fortuna, became Rome's 7th king through marriage. On the eve of June 23, bonfires were lit to Fortuna and Pomona to invite souls of the recently departed to celebrate. Wealthy and servants alike, in a festival of decorated boats and along the banks of the river Tiber, enjoyed feasting, dancing, drinking and gambling.

July

July 6 & 14, Days of Fortuna Muliebris, celebrated a 5th century BCE feminist temple dedicated to the women of Rome, and run completely by women. The first priestess was the mother of Roman warrior, and later soldier-of-Fortune against Rome, Coriolanus. The temple celebrated an event of peace-keeping so dramatic that Shakespeare made it the subject of a play by the same name, which was recently brought to the screen in a violently gripping, contemporary retelling. Coriolanus refused to negotiate with men, but relented to his mother's and wife's pleas for peace.

July 30, Day of Fortuna Huiusque Diei (fortune of the present day), solemnly dedicated a temple in 101 BCE in thanks for a day of divine assistance. The course of events was changed for Roman warriors, one summer day, when they captured Teutobod, king of the Teutons. Rome was so terrorized by tribal warriors, and the clamorous, prophesying, murderous female priestesses who accompanied them into battle, that they gave it a name: terror Cimbricus. The 25-foot-high temple statue has a slightly open-mouthed, lifelike expression, and watchful, wide-open eyes.

August

August 13, Day of Fortuna Equestris, was a temple vowed by Roman horse-mounted knight, Flaccus, in 173 BCE in thanks for success in battle. Flaccus was a confident leader who bent rules that he found inconvenient, which resulted in Flaccus's expulsion from his preferred career path. Legend tells that, in building the temple, Flaccus told his men to steal marble from a Roman temple to Juno (Fortuna's mother). Within a year, Flaccus and his two sons were dead. Roman coins circulated in 186 CE show Goddess *Fortuna Mananti* (to abiding fortune) guiding a horse.

September

September 27, Day of Fortuna Reducis marked the safe return of the Emperor Caesar Augustus, to Rome from overseas, with an altar built in 19 BCE. The altar was a formal focal point in Rome, in honor of their leader's successful role in the final conflict with Queen Cleopatra and Mark Antony, the conquering of Egypt by Rome and the adoption of Egypt as part of the Roman Empire. Statues of Isis-Fortuna, along with other Isis-syncretized Roman Goddesses, were created in first century CE Rome, along with a new Roman fascination for all things Egyptian.

October

October 3 to 12, Days of Fortuna Reducis (or Redux) were officially known as the Augustalia or Ludi Augustales (the Augustan Games), a celebration of Emperor Caesar Augustus' birthday on October 12. In the tradition of Egyptian pharaohs, Augustus was later deified, and temples to Fortuna Augustus built within the Roman Empire. The Augustalia (held around the same time of year as contemporary "Pagan Pride" events) was an energetic, festive celebration of the arts, sports and competitive events like chariot races, musical and athletic contests.

November

November 13, Day of Fortuna Primigenia, was most likely named for one of three temples known collectively in Rome as the Tres Fortunae. The two temples to Fortuna Publica (dedicated in April and May) may also have been in this complex; however, there appears to be some conflicting information regarding this topic. Primigenia refers to the bearing of children of the Roman gens, or lineage of Roman citizenry, and Fortuna's role as either the first-born daughter of Jupiter, or the first daughter who bore children (Minerva being a chaste daughter of Jupiter).

December

December 1, Day of Fortuna Muliebris, was a third holiday dedicated to "Womanly Fortune". The Temple of Fortuna Muliebris was not only run by an all-female priestesshood, the services were only open to women. Some sources state that individual men were allowed, by invitation only, yet this seems to have been the exception if, indeed, it ever happened at all. Due to its secrecy, the rituals of this cult are not available because they do not seem to have been written down. Rites may have been similar to contemporary, women-only NeoPagan Goddess circles. December 15, Day of Fortuna Redux, opened the altar of Augustus' safe return from overseas to the general public. Members of the Roman populace would request the blessings of Fortuna Redux, as a Goddess of the Emperor Augustus' people, for the safe return of their own family members and loved ones who were away from home, in distant travels or overseas. Anyone and everyone were allowed to pray to this, then new, aspect of the Goddess Fortuna. The Augustan Era became known as the Pax Romana, or the age of peace, in contrast to Rome's war history.

PRAISES & SUPPLICATIONS

An act of kindness for someone who is miserable
is like a gift to Fortuna.

Andromache's Plea
691 from *Troades (the Trojan Women)*
by Lucius Annaeus Seneca (Seneca the Younger)

SPRING SEASON

A Prayer for the Path

Goddess, who is with us in our public and private lives,
In ancient times, Pagan people were of the countryside,
Planting seeds, tending crops and reaping the harvest;
Honoring divine relationships of earth, sun, rain and air.

In those times, the Goddess was honored in the cities,
Included in public temples, events, rituals, processions,
Influencing the affairs of all men, women and children,
Of all classes and ages, throughout the ancient world.

In our times, a few Pagan people are in the countryside,
And a few are here and there in the cities and suburbs,
Carefully tended with Your protection and blessings,
As the caretakers of Your ancient and divine legacy.

Please continue to protect and bless your children,
As equal and respected members of the community,
Help us grow and spread the word to friendly people,
Of this peaceful, spiritual belief in the world today.

And so it is blessed, favorable, fruitful and fortunate,
Goddess Fortuna!

Blessed be.

A Prayer for the Coming of Spring

Today is a wondrous day! The first shoots of spring rise from earth
And the fiery glow of the sun begins to warm the activities of our day.
We praise the sun, with candles, and with hearth fires and bonfires
As our small yet humble mirror of the power of the mighty solar deity.

With this warmth, the earth is healed of its winter chill and hibernation,
Our homes are cleansed of the dust, cobwebs, and stillness of winter
As we welcome the Goddess, the maiden, the bride and a new birth
Of spring to our lives, our homes, our gardens and rejoice in the day!

And so it is blessed, favorable, fruitful and fortunate,
Goddess Fortuna Virginalis!

Blessed be.

A Prayer for Spirituality

Goddess, who is with us one day at a time,
You know that our days can be very busy
Sometimes it is difficult to find the time for spirituality
And we give thanks when our days continue profitably
So that we may continue to receive your blessings.

When we are hurried to complete our daily agenda
Sometimes we forget to take the time for prayer
Please forgive us, and in those times, we pray for your divine guidance
So that we may understand the grand plan for each day
And create space for our blessings and meditations
Through careful planning of each and every day.

Allow us to stretch ourselves and become efficient
To refrain from wasting time and expressing negativity
And to be able to clearly tell the difference in the present moment.
Please send Your Goddess power to protect our spirituality
In those times when we feel overpowered by duties.

And so it is blessed, favorable, fruitful and fortunate,
Goddess Fortuna Huiusque Diei!

Blessed be.

Prayer for Intelligence and Fellowship of Humankind

As we propel our future generations into the age of Aquarius
We reach out in friendship and enlightened communications
In this wonderful new era of global love and relationships
And we aspire to intelligence and fellowship of all humankind.

And so it is blessed, favorable, fruitful and fortunate,
Goddess Fortuna!

Blessed be.

Prayer for Thoughtful Silence

Goddess, who is with us in our public lives
You know that at times, in the heat of conversation
When we hear another human speak powerfully
On a subject that sparks our personal emotions
We are tempted to respond back passionately
And to say things which we wish we had not.

When we do not stop and allow ourselves
The luxury of becoming calm and contemplative,
Please send us a gentle reminder to take care
And enough time to absorb and understand.
Allow our emotions to drift away peacefully
And to release any negativity in our beliefs.

Even as the conversation rolls and turns
And others jab and thrust their opinions wildly,
Give us the humility to wait, watch and learn,
With our faith that we may contribute value
To our communications in our own silence
So that our mirror reflects a shining light.

And so it is blessed, favorable, fruitful and fortunate,
Goddess Fortuna Publica!

Blessed be.

Prayer for Motherhood

In this season of new growth, when our ancestors prepared for the labor
In the fields, for the preparation of the land and planting of the seeds
For the preservation of their lives throughout the year, we are reminded
Of the work of the mothers who bring to light new generations of family.

Please allow our labors to be safe, simple, productive and manageable
Permit us to balance our emotions, exercise, and nutrition effectively
So that generations in our families, and generosity in our neighborhoods
May graciously and happily receive the gift of a healthy, new child to love.

And so it is blessed, favorable, fruitful and fortunate,
Goddess Fortuna Primigenia!

Blessed be.

Prayer to Realize our Wishes and Dreams

In these days of increasing daylight,
we have passed into the illumination,
To the season of looking outward with anticipation;
we know our dreams.
Our actions demonstrate our intentions
of reaching to higher aspirations;
Our greatest hopes, our visions of our future
and other lighthearted events.

In these months ahead, when we see the light
of the sun throughout the day
We revisit sacred goals and find what we need
radiating within ourselves.
Please bless us on the roads to realizing
our dreams and spiritual desires.
May this realization glow along with us;
the brilliant light of the growing day.

And so it is blessed, favorable, fruitful and fortunate,
Goddess Fortuna!

Blessed be.

Prayer for Knowledge

As we journey through this unprecedented age
of global communication,
Let us remember the fine distinction
between information and knowledge.
Please guide us to learn the individual limits
of our abilities to learn, retain,
And forgive us when we grow tired
of filling our cups with facts and figures.

Give us your Goddess blessings
so that we may know the divine pathway
To true knowledge that comes from
all our life experiences and friendships
As well as traditional studies
and global communications we all appreciate.
Send us your guiding light to illuminate
the way to the greatest knowledge.

And so it is blessed, favorable, fruitful and fortunate,
Goddess Fortuna!

Blessed be.

Prayer at the Equinox of Spring

Here in the Equinox of spring,
as the balance is tenuously created between night and day,
Dark and light, dusk and dawn;
for a brief moment in time all is still and the scales of justice
Are perfectly aligned in equilibrium,
as we anticipate the harvest we will reap in the autumn,
The next time we experience this exquisite
yet transitory astronomical influence in our lives.

We pause, during this space in time,
to give thanks for seed we will sow once again on earth,
For the ample opportunity to experience
regrowth and renewal beginning at the spring equinox
And growing in the brighter, warmer and
pleasant months ahead. We join together in praise
And plant our hopes, dreams and thanks for
this new morning in the brilliance of the daylight!

And so it is blessed, favorable, fruitful and fortunate,
Goddess Fortuna!

Blessed be.

Prayer of the Head of Household

You who inspires us to be good providers for our homes,
I pray to You, and I honor my household in fidelity of heart.

You, whose necklaces and riches have been gently removed,
I prepare You, and I honor my household in fidelity of heart.

You who shall be cleansed and purified of all transgressions,
I protect You, and I honor my household in fidelity of heart.

You who once again receives the gifts of beauty and wealth,
I return You, and I honor my household in fidelity of heart.

You who fills Your cornucopia with beautiful blooms,
I bathe for You, and I honor my household in fidelity of heart.

You who inhales the sweet smell of incense and sacred herbs,
I give to You, and I honor my household in fidelity of heart.

You who imbibes of the crushed poppies in milk and honey,
I serve to You, and I honor my household in fidelity of heart.

You with reputation refreshed, nourished, and sanctified,
I honor You, and I honor my household in fidelity of heart.

I honor You and my household in this invocation and in release.
I honor You and my household in fidelity, harmony and peace.

And so it is blessed, favorable, fruitful and fortunate,
Goddess Fortuna Virilis!

Blessed be.

Prayer for Safety and Protection of our Public Image

You who are with us in public
and gives us safe harbor,
From all life's uncertain moments,
Like a friendly neighbor,
Please come to us at all those times
So we'll know what to do.

Keep us from naive foolishness
And we will all thank You.
Sometimes our friends have bad ideas
And we want to say "no",
But when our words are not well heard
We'll know it's time to go.

And when the day at last is done,
The sun has gone to rest,
We'll sleep soundly and peacefully
And know we've done our best
To keep the peace and keep our friends
No matter what they do.

The choice is ours to stay or go
And our strength comes from You!

And so it is blessed, favorable, fruitful and fortunate,
Goddess Fortuna Publica!

Blessed be.

Prayer for Energy and Enthusiasm

Oh Fortuna, whose Goddess influence we experience
Under the sun and in daylight,
Harmonious, and yet different from the lunar Goddess,
We welcome Your presence.

The sun shines on us, giving fiery brilliance in our day
Radiating, glowing, pulsating,
Communicating with all our senses in divine luminosity
Horizon to mid-sky to horizon.

Today, we honor the empowerment of the mighty sun,
Brightest star to mother earth,
And allow the solar energy to penetrate our inner being
Bringing gifts of enthusiasm.

And so it is blessed, favorable, fruitful and fortunate,
Goddess Fortuna!

Blessed be.

Prayer of a Parent

Our children are born into the world
and create a new role for us as parents,
Filling our lives with health and safety
concerns leading up to their birth,
And continuing; as we share life's lessons
and watch them grow each day,
Seeing them learn to make choices, decisions
and share their innocent love.

Allow us to provide gentle guidance,
along with our patience and acceptance.
Please grant us faith, love and endurance
as an example that can be copied,
And when the time finally arrives that our children
come into their adult years
Let our love continue strong, generous
and respectful of their independence.

And so it is blessed, favorable, fruitful and fortunate,
Goddess Fortuna, who turns the wheel!

Blessed be.

Prayer for Stability

In these times which can seem to be very uncertain and insecure,
Affecting our finances, emotions, safety, health, and relationships,
Sometimes in an absolutely enormous variety of manifestations
Which can overwhelm and confuse us in making our life's choices,

Please allow us to separate the different pathways instability takes
So that we may realize more clearly our ability to uncover, claim
And create within ourselves to project into our consciousness
As a gift to You, a gift to ourselves, and a gift to our communities:

Stability in our finances
Stability in our emotions
Stability in our health
Stability in our relationships

And may we take the greatest pride in our accomplishments today.

And so it is blessed, favorable, fruitful and fortunate,
Goddess Fortuna!

Blessed be.

SUMMER SEASON

Prayer for Romance and Love

Goddess, who brings forth friendship, passion and romance,
We engage in love, with all the colors of the spring flowers.

We engage in love and passion in red.
We engage in love and communication in orange.
We engage in love and friendship in yellow.

We engage in love and fidelity in green.
We engage in love and friendship in pink.
We engage in love and kisses in blue.

We engage in love and spirituality in indigo.
We engage in love and protection in purple.
We engage in love and purity in white.

We engage in love, we are loved, and request Your blessings.

And so it is blessed, favorable, fruitful and fortunate,
Goddess Fortuna-Venus!

Blessed be.

Prayer for Belief in the Magic of Miracles

As we go throughout our daily lives we can see miracles of nature:
The new growth and beautiful flowers of spring
The long days and ripened fruits in the summer
The abundance of produce harvested in autumn
The perfect geometries of snowflakes in winter
And we are amazed at the divine energies that created this world.

Sometimes we feel small in comparison to this grandiose magic:
As people, we also wish for wondrous change
As humans, we also have dreams and visions
As men and women, we also complete projects
As mortals, we also need shelter and protection
And we ask Your Goddess blessings our own magic and miracles.

As we are reminded of Your miracles in the natural world of magic
Please remind us of our own abilities to create miracles and magic.

And so it is blessed, favorable, fruitful and fortunate,
Goddess Fortuna!

Blessed be.

Prayer for a Profitable Business

Goddess of good fortune, You know the necessity of income;
For our housing
For our meals
For the finer things in life.

In moments of leisure, we dream of magic and miracles;
To inherit a house
To win the lottery
To marry into great wealth.

But, for most of us, that money comes from our business;
The money flows
The money ebbs
The balance like ocean waves.

And in equilibrium, we honor the higher and divine powers;
With sacred prayer
With scented air
With bay and cleansing water.

Please bring success, and allow our businesses to profit;
An income greater
A debt is smaller
An inspiration to continue.

And so it is blessed, favorable, fruitful and fortunate,
Goddess Fortuna!

Blessed be.

Prayer for a Happy Baby

On the path to childbirth, family and friends wonder
Will she be a girl? Will he be a boy?

And what colors should we select for the baby?
Pink or blue? Neutral or yellow?

And what clothes will the mother be wearing?
Fashionable? Comfortable?

And how will the act of birth be accomplished?
Long and laborious? Short and sweet?

And which parent will the baby most favor?
The mother's eyes? The father's strength?

What will shape the baby's little personality?
Sun sign astrology? Parent's heredity?

How soon will the baby learn their lessons?
When to talk? When to walk?

In this extended excitement of expectations
Worries, concerns, questions, curiosity

Please grant this baby happiness and acceptance.
Love and laughter, joy and wonder

Perfect health and prosperity within the family.
Perfect love and acceptance in the community.

And so it is blessed, favorable, fruitful and fortunate,
Goddess Fortuna Primigenia!

Blessed be.

Prayer for Summer

Today is a fabulous day! The fruits are formed and growing
And the fiery glow of the sun brings heat to the longer day.
We praise the season, with dance, with picnics in the park
And the celebrations of romance, love, fertility and fidelity.
And so it is blessed, favorable, fruitful and fortunate,
Goddess Fors Fortuna!

Blessed be.

Prayer for a Happy Marriage

As we leave the home with memories of our own childhoods
And embrace a new life with the one that we have chosen,
Prepare for our futures, our finances, and our new family,
Many adventures and hidden pathways will open for us.

Goddess, we thank You for the marvelous opportunity
That You have granted us from the moment we met
And the love and communication that guided us
And blessed us to bring us where we are now.

Please be with us in our moments of love
Please guide us in our uncertain times
Please bless us now, in the future
As you have blessed us before.

Let us remember our dreams,
Our beliefs and our faith
And give us strength,
Always, as we join

And seal this,
Our love,
With a
kiss.

And so it is blessed, favorable, fruitful and fortunate,
Goddess Fortuna Virilis and Fortuna Virginalis!

Blessed be.

Prayer to Overcome Difficulties

At some point in our lives,
we will encounter situations that seem daunting.
Whether they be smaller difficulties
like miscommunication between friends,
Or larger issues such as illness, unemployment
or the loss of a loved one.

Please help us to remember
that the wheel of life turns in a circular pattern,
That we will find a way to travel the path
from past to future, from the bottom
To the top of the wheel and discover
how to become stronger in adversity.

And so it is blessed, favorable, fruitful and fortunate,
Goddess Fortuna, who turns the wheel!

Blessed be.

Prayer for Wealth and Prosperity at the Summer Solstice

Goddess, who brings wealth to the poor and underprivileged,
You know well the financial difficulties that are faced by us daily.
At this magical time of empowering, golden sunlight,
Please bring a golden magical light to our sources of prosperity
So they may be rejuvenated and filled with wealth.

As people we create the economic cycles,
Which we pray will turn to benefit us at this time, and
Those of us who need more than we now have,
Pray for Your divine guidance.
Please forgive any of our actions which may have
Contributed to our current financial situation,

Allow us to become gainfully employed,
Or otherwise receiving our fair share of wealth,
And learn how to work through any interference if it has
Interrupted our cycle of prosperity.
Please send Your Goddess power of financial wealth
On your sacred day at the solstice of summer.

And so it is blessed, favorable, fruitful and fortunate,
Goddess Fors Fortuna!

Blessed be.

Prayer of Healing of Mother Earth and Ourselves

Goddess, who brings health to newborn children and mothers,
You know well the difficulties that are faced by us in our health.
At this time our earth mother is in need of healing.
As people have discovered the vast wealth of resources
and ways in which to use them,
sometimes we make mistakes.

Please forgive us our mistakes
so that we may move forward and learn
how to heal the damage which has been
done to our precious mother.
Please send Your Goddess powers of healing
in our time of need.

And so it is blessed, favorable, fruitful and fortunate,
Goddess Fortuna Primigenia!

Blessed be.

Prayer for Courage in Public Speaking

Goddess, who empowers us to speak with our minds, and with our hearts,
You know that sometimes we should take a stand.
Sometimes it is difficult to say the things we know we must,
Especially if those who listen may be strong and disagree.
When we are worried, sometimes we are also silent.

Please forgive us, and in those silent times,
We pray for Your divine guidance
So that we may find the courage to speak
Confidently, clearly, with meaningful words
Worthy of consideration.

Allow us to express ourselves with strength and dignity,
Lift us above pettiness, finger-pointing and arguments,
To voice our words in the most uplifting way possible.
Please send Your Goddess power to speak through us.

And so it is blessed, favorable, fruitful and fortunate,
Goddess Fortuna Muliebris!

Blessed be.

Prayer for Peace

Goddess, who empowers us to speak with our minds, and with our hearts,
We pray for peace, with all the colors of the earth and sky,

We pray for peace with strength and power in red.
We pray for peace with vitality, potency and courage in orange.
We pray for peace with intelligence and knowledge in yellow.
We pray for peace with abundance and love in green.
We pray for peace with communication, and spirituality in blue.
We pray for peace through synthesis and inner wisdom in indigo.
We pray for peace with spirituality and guidance in purple.

We pray for peace with enlightenment in white.
We pray for peace on the path to our future in gold.
We pray for peace with persistence and resolve in gray.
We pray for peace and see a sparkle for hope in silver.
We pray for peace and see the changes occurring in black.
We are all grounded with resolve for the path of peace as we have chosen.

And so it is blessed, favorable, fruitful and fortunate,
Goddess Fortuna Muliebris!

Blessed be.

Prayer for Communication

Goddess, who is with us in our private lives
You know that sometimes we feel strong emotions
Sometimes it is difficult to know why we feel as we do
And how to express ourselves to each other calmly
So that we may continue to live together in harmony.

When we are confused with our own emotions
Sometimes we say things that we do not intend,
Please forgive us, and in those times, we pray for your divine guidance
So that we may understand the reasons for our emotions
And have pride in the way that we express ourselves
Through carefully chosen, calm actions and words

Allow us to express our shared emotions appropriately,
To refrain from expressing our discordant emotions,
And to be able to clearly tell the difference at a moment's notice.
Please send Your Goddess power to protect us in our private lives
In those times when we feel overpowered by emotion.

And so it is blessed, favorable, fruitful and fortunate,
Goddess Fortuna Privata!

Blessed be.

Prayer of the Present Day

You who are with us every day
and one day at a time,
Some days we have difficulties
and some days are just fine.

We do good deeds for those who are
Less fortunate than we,
And ask for Your Goddess guidance;
The better path to see.

If we have wronged someone we knew
In days that passed before,
Let us now make amends today
And even up the score.

When we achieve a great success,
We celebrate with You
And give You praise for Your wisdom,
And for all that You do.

When evening comes and day is done
We look forward to when
We may awake, and greet the day,
And start over again!

And so it is blessed, favorable, fruitful and fortunate,
Goddess Fortuna Huiusque Diei, for good Goddess fortune of the present day!

Blessed Be.

AUTUMN SEASON

Prayer of the Autumn Harvest

This is the time of year when we see our Autumn harvest;
When the vegetables are ripe and the grain is tall.
We ready ourselves for the hard work and reap this bounty,
Preparing to bake the first bread of prosperity this year.

We thank You for the abundance of this botanical cornucopia
And we are amazed at the magnitude of Your divine generosity
As we ask for Your continued protection in the year ahead
And praise You as we prepare to move into the cold season.

And so it is blessed, favorable, fruitful and fortunate,
Goddess Fortuna!

Blessed Be.

Prayer for Effective Leadership

Our world has changed much since the time of ancient Rome.
Sometimes it is difficult to know who is leader and who is follower.
Our roles change constantly,
from work or school to home,
from job to job
And our prayer is twofold, depending on which character we play:

As a leader, a manager, a parent, we pray to lead graciously,
To respect that everyone is valuable; to be available and on time;
When praise is deserving, to give it abundantly and with sincerity,
When direction is required, to give it quietly, privately, and with dignity.

As a follower, an employee, a child, we pray to follow respectfully
To realize that everyone has responsibilities;
to be patient and cooperative;
When we have done well, to receive our praise humbly
and with gratitude,
When we make mistakes, to admit them willingly, so that we may learn.

And when we change from one role to another, please give us strength
And guidance so that we may not be overly humble, nor overly proud,
And willing to move forward in harmony with all of our communities
As we enjoy all the ways to play
this great and wonderful game called "life"!

And so it is blessed, favorable, fruitful and fortunate,
Fortuna Equestris!

Blessed be.

Prayer of the Holly and the Ivy for Love Between a Man and a Woman

The Holly and the Ivy, when they are both full-grown
Of all the trees that are in the wood, may these grow to become one.
The rising of the sun, and the running of the deer,
The turning of the Goddess wheel brings new mysteries each year!

The holly bears a blossom, white as the lily flower
As the ivy springs up from the earth to make each other lovers.
The rising of the sun, and the running of the deer,
The turning of the Goddess wheel brings new mysteries each year!

The holly bears a berry as red as any blood
As the ivy grows most steadfastly even through the rains and flood.
The rising of the sun, and the running of the deer,
The turning of the Goddess wheel brings new mysteries each year!

The holly bears a prickle as sharp as any thorn
As the ivy wears her glorious mane after all the trees are shorn.
The rising of the sun, and the running of the deer,
The turning of the Goddess wheel brings new mysteries each year!

The holly bears a bark, bitter as any gall
As the ivy mirrors back his love; summer, winter, spring and fall.
The rising of the sun, and the running of the deer,
The turning of the Goddess wheel brings new mysteries each year!

The holly and the ivy, when they are both full-grown
Of all the trees that are in the wood, may these grow to become one.
The rising of the sun, and the running of the deer,
The turning of the Goddess wheel brings new mysteries each year!

And so it is blessed, favorable, fruitful and fortunate,
Goddess Fortuna, who turns the Goddess wheel!

Blessed Be.

Prayer for Health

With the strength of the sun we give praise for health,
With the strength of our well-being is our wealth,
With the strength of our minds illness has no stealth,
We give praise to the Goddess for health!

In the sun we give thanks for our health and strength,
In the sun we have hope our lives have long length,
In the sun we give praise as our prayer is sent,
We give praise to the Goddess for strength!

For our health and our strength we get from the sun,
For our health is what makes our days safe and fun,
For our health continues when the day is done,
And we give Goddess praise in the sun!

Praise to the sun!
Praise to our strength!
Praise to our health!

And so it is blessed, favorable, fruitful and fortunate,
Goddess Fortuna Salutaris!

Blessed be.

Prayer of a Student

Goddess, who brings good fortune and leadership,
You know well that study and work can lead to success.
Please give us the strength and willpower
To move forward in our studies and ask questions freely.

Please send us assistance when we do not understand,
Bless us with kind and knowledgeable instructors,
And friends and companions who are like-minded,
Especially when temptations arrive to distract us.

Please guide us to take responsibility for ourselves,
Help us to remember to balance play and study,
Keep a clear vision of our goals, pass our tests,
And to deliver all our work on time as our best effort.

And so it is blessed, favorable, fruitful and fortunate,
Goddess Fortuna!

Blessed be.

Prayer of Solitary Spirituality

In this season of the virgin, as many of us go about
our spirituality in solitary beliefs
Grant us peace of mind and inspiration in our daily affairs,
both at work and at home.
Allow others to understand that our solitude is not the same
as living in loneliness,
And that our lives are at least as full of love and happiness
as couples and families.

Please grant us freedom from discrimination by congregations
in our neighborhoods
Allow us respect for our own personal labors, equality of salary,
a pleasant place to work,
And when we come home at the end of the day to our small
and simple pleasures,
Let us give thanks to the Goddess for Her attendance
and all that She has provided for us.

And so it is blessed, favorable, fruitful and fortunate,
Goddess Fortuna!

Blessed be.

Prayer of a Worker

In this season of harvest, when our ancestors realized
the results of their labor
In the fields, with the gathering of the fruits of the vine in preparation for
Preserving by canning, by fermenting, or by other way,
we are reminded
Of our work by which we provide for our homes and
families through the year.

Please allow our labors to be satisfying, productive
and compensated fairly
Permit us to balance our labor, home
and recreational activities effectively
So that harmony in our homes, and generosity
in our friendships is accomplished
Each and every day in the sun, and each and every night,
under the moonbeams.

And so it is blessed, favorable, fruitful and fortunate,
Goddess Fortuna-Venus!

Blessed be.

Prayer for the Equinox of Autumn

Here in the Equinox of autumn, as the balance
is tenuously created between day and night,
Light and dark, life and death; for a brief moment in time
all is still and the scales of justice
Are perfectly aligned in equilibrium, and we remember
the seeds which we planted in the spring,
At the last time we remembered this exquisite yet transitory
astronomical influence in our lives.

We pause, during this space in time, to give thanks
for what we have been able to accomplish
Throughout the summer, which has provided us
ample opportunity for regrowth and renewal
In preparation for the darker, colder and stormier months ahead.
We gather together our work,
Our hopes, our dreams and give thanks for the careful planning
which ensures our survival.

And so it is blessed, favorable, fruitful and fortunate,
Goddess Fortuna!

Blessed be.

Prayer for In-Laws and Extended Family

We are born to parents divinely selected
for reasons we may never understand,
And, as we grow and our world changes;
sometimes internally within the family,
And always externally; as we leave the home
and meet with new friends,
Including our online friends, we begin to develop
choices in our affiliations.

With these choices come new opportunities,
new lessons, and new difficulties.
Please grant us faith, love and endurance
in our new friendships and liaisons,
And also in the most permanent of lifelong relationship choices,
our marriages.
May this love also strengthen our bonds with our in-laws
and extended families.

And so it is blessed, favorable, fruitful and fortunate,
Goddess Isis-Fortuna!

Blessed be.

Prayer for Safety of Our Loved Ones

The world has always been a mixed blessing
of both safe and dangerous situations,
And when our loved ones are away from us,
we feel concerns over their well-being.
We send our psychic support regularly in an effort
to keep security concerns controlled,
Both for ourselves and loved ones at home,
and also for those temporarily away from us.

Please, Goddess, take care of us, our families,
our friends, and support our situations
So that our daily affairs are pleasant to all concerned,
in all ways and also in all places,
As the balance of our lives is affected not only
by those we know well; it is influenced by
Those who come into our lives and bring about change.
May these changes be beneficial.

And so it is blessed, favorable, fruitful and fortunate,
Goddess Fortuna Redux!

Blessed be.

Prayer to Cope with Separation

Sometimes in our lives, we find ourselves
separated from our loved ones and friends,
Either through personal choice, family relocations
or forces temporarily beyond our control.
During these times we are tested in our faith, our beliefs,
our honesty, and our loyalty,
And, many times, these tests come our direction
when we feel least prepared to face them.

It is in these times that we find moments of doubt
in our faith, beliefs, honesty and loyalty,
And even in our own motives and reasons for existence
on this planet, Our Mother Earth.
Please bring us the strength to trust ourselves,
that we are here for a very vital reason,
And allow our separations to strengthen our bonds,
and discover beneficial ways to cope.

No! Let us not sink into despair, questions, lack of faith,
lies, deceit, blame or even betrayal.
Lift us above our worst fears and let Your Goddess Light
show us the way to communicate,
To bring us out of ourselves and our personal worries
and realize we are not alone in this.
Let us reach across this void, speak or write;
and be assured our messages are appreciated.

And so it is blessed, favorable, fruitful and fortunate,
Goddess Fortuna Redux!

Blessed be.

Prayer for Justice

The world has always been a mixed blessing
of both just and unjust situations,
And although we try to live our lives well,
doing good deed for the unfortunate,
Taking care of our loved ones and looking out
for our own beneficial opportunities,
We do not know why the scales of justice
are not always balanced in our favor.

Please, Goddess, take care of us, our families,
our friends, and give guidance
So that we may better understand Your divine pathway
to justice and fairness,
And let us be lead away from the negativity that
causes us to doubt your wisdom,
And light the way to a better future,
with the knowledge that we have acquired.

And so it is blessed, favorable, fruitful and fortunate,
Goddess Fortuna!

Blessed be.

Prayer for Our Ancestors

Through the veil of life we remember our dead,
Through the veil comes love from our ancestors' bed,
Through the veil comes acceptance, joy and not dread.
May the Goddess bring peace to our dead.

In our life we visit our dead through the veil,
In our life we recall each ancestor's tale,
In our life we have pride so we will not fail,
May the Goddess bring peace through the veil.

May our dead use the veil to visit us in life,
May our dead feel relief of their cares and strife,
May our dead feel our love like husband and wife,
May the Goddess bring peace in our life.

Peace to our dead!
Peace through the veil!
Peace in our life!

And so it is blessed, favorable, fruitful and fortunate,
Goddess Fortuna Privata!

Blessed be.

WINTER SEASON

Prayer for Enlightenment

In these days of increasing darkness,
we have crossed through the veil,
Looked at ourselves and our ancestors,
and faced our deepest fears unafraid.
Our thoughts turn inwards to our own difficulties,
or economic situations,
Our health, our loved ones who are away
from us, and serious concerns.

At these times when we think mainly of lightening
ourselves of our burdens
We discover enlightenment is what is most needed
to bring us out of ourselves.
Please grant us the pathway to enlightenment
and deliver us from introspection
May this enlightenment light the way to a brighter future
for us and our community.

And so it is blessed, favorable, fruitful and fortunate,
Goddess Fortuna!

Blessed be.

Prayer for Baby's Health

Mother envisions health for her baby,
Seeing good futures that she hopes will be,
Hoping the deities all will agree.
We praise the Goddess for the baby!

Baby's nutrition and health from mother,
Giving equally to son or daughter,
Wishing for each one long life and laughter.
We praise the Goddess for the mother!

From mother to baby we pray for health,
From mother's well-being brings new-born wealth,
From mother the strength and life-force does spilth.
We praise the Goddess for love and health!

Praise for mother!
Praise for baby!
Praise for the health!

And so it is blessed, favorable, fruitful and fortunate,
Goddess Fortuna Primigenia!

Blessed be.

Prayer for the Hearth and Home

As the weather becomes colder,
the days grow shorter; the nights longer,
The harvest, which we stored so recently,
begins to appear on our tables.
Our study, work, relationships and
our recreational activities move indoors,
And those who work outdoors welcome
the warmth of hearth and home.

At this time of year we are closely gathered
together in peaceful activities,
Seeking ways to cooperate, enjoy and bring
happiness to our loved ones.
Please grant us the patience, love
And generosity to brighten our hearth.
May our hearth and home be a place
of peace and security this season.

And so it is blessed, favorable, fruitful and fortunate,
Goddess Fortuna!

Blessed be.

Prayer of Thanks and Peace

Goddess, who empowers us
to speak with our minds,
and with our hearts,
We give thanks for peace,
with all the colors of the earth and sky,

We give thanks for peace with a strong voice in red.
We give thanks for peace with intelligence in orange.
We give thanks for peace with great success in yellow.
We give thanks for peace with all our love in green.

We give thanks for peace with our spirituality in blue.
We give thanks for peace with wisdom in indigo.
We give thanks for peace with guidance in purple.
We give thanks for peace with enlightenment in white.

We give thanks for peace in the sunlight in gold.
We give thanks for peace with resolve in gray.
We give thanks for peace under the stars in silver.
We give thanks for peace as the change occurs in black.

We give thanks to those who listen and follow the path of peace.

And so it is blessed, favorable, fruitful and fortunate,
Goddess Fortuna Muliebris!

Blessed be.

Prayer for Friendship

As we gather inside the home to share love with our family,
We look forward to festive celebrations of the holiday season
That we share with people outside our personal households.
Let us remember our friends and welcome them into our lives.

And so it is blessed, favorable, fruitful and fortunate,
Goddess Fortuna!

Blessed be.

Prayer for Safe Return

The world is a very large place and,
even in these days of global communications,
There are times when, as people, we must travel
far away from our loved ones.
We send our psychic support to our loved ones regularly
when we are separated
By physical distances in the maps of the physical realms
of our shared existences.

Please, Goddess, take care of us, our families,
our friends, and send Your blessings
So that we may all live our lives well,
wherever we may physically find ourselves,
And, with Your blessings, when the time is right,
bring our loved ones home to us,
Safely, securely, with love, trust, understanding
and faith in Your protective powers.

And so it is blessed, favorable, fruitful and fortunate,
Goddess Fortuna Redux!

Blessed be.

Prayer of Celebration at the Winter Solstice

Goddess, who is with us in our public and our private lives,
Now light of day is shortest and darkness of night longest.
We ready ourselves for the festivities of the winter season,
In the coldest and harshest weather conditions of the year.

Once again, the wheel has turned; we gift and celebrate;
And thank You for the opportunity to provide joy to others,
And ask You for your divine guidance in our relationships,
As we give and attend parties and events to end this year.

And so it is blessed, favorable, fruitful and fortunate,
Goddess Fortuna!

Blessed be.

Prayer for the Coming Year at the Winter Solstice

Goddess, who is with us in our public and our private lives,
Now light of day is shortest and darkness of night longest.
We ready ourselves for the festivities of the winter season,
In the coldest and harshest weather conditions of the year.

As the holiday season of winter begins, the weather's chill again familiar,
We are ready for the festivities and events, with decorations and gifts
Renewing acquaintances with distant relatives, co-workers and friends,
As the reality of the darkest day of the year has finally arrived to greet us.

Once again, the wheel has turned; we gift and celebrate;
And thank You for the opportunity to provide joy to others,
And thank You for your divine guidance in our relationships,
As we give and attend parties and events to end this year.

We look forward to the celebrations,
in the heart of the rain, snow and hail.
We know that the light will grow stronger
and longer as we break through
To the other side and look ahead toward
the planting and growth of spring.
Please help us to renew ourselves
and our world for the coming season.

And so it is blessed, favorable, fruitful and fortunate,
Goddess Fortuna, who turns the wheel!

Blessed be.

Prayer for Victory and Success

Goddess, who brings victory and success in competition,
You know well all my preparations, practice and study.
As I enter into this competition, I ask for Your blessings.
Please bring me the abilities, words, decisions, actions,
That I have envisioned bringing about the desired results.
Help me choose the direction to take the brightest path,
And protect me from all harm.

Regardless of the score, salary, or grade at the day's end,
Allow me the fortitude to continue learning and improving
How to further develop my plans, career, methods and goals
And reach higher, better, and impressively in the year ahead,
So that I may bring pleasure and pride to my own loved ones.
Please send Your Goddess powers of victory and success,
Today and every day.

And so it is blessed, favorable, fruitful and fortunate,
Goddess Fortuna!

Blessed be.

Prayer of Renewal for the Coming Year

As the holiday season of winter begins,
the weather's chill again familiar,
We prepare for the festivities and events,
selecting and wrapping presents
Renewing acquaintances with distant relatives,
co-workers and friends,
As the reality of the darkest day of the year
rapidly approaches to greet us.

We look forward to the celebrations, in the heart
of the rain, snow and hail.
We know that the light will grow stronger and longer
as we break through
To the other side and look ahead toward
the planting and growth of spring.
Please help us to renew ourselves
and our world for the coming season.

And so it is blessed, favorable, fruitful and fortunate,
Goddess Fortuna!

Blessed be.

Prayer for the New Year

Goddess Fortuna, in all your aspects of this coming year,
As the light of day grows and darkness of night diminishes,
Once again, the wheel has turned; we peer into the future,
And we thank you with gifts of celebration and prayer.

As the New Year approaches, we request a triple blessing,
A blessing for good health, a blessing for prosperity wealth,
and a blessing for all the happiness that You may provide,
for our today, for our tomorrow, and throughout the new year.

And so it is blessed, favorable, fruitful and fortunate,
Goddess Fortuna, in all Your wonderful aspects!

Blessed be.

Prayer after the New Year

All the gifts of the season have become earthly possessions,
The festivities and celebrations of last year recent memories,
Through the winter's chill, the slow drum beat of growing sun
Warms the still and silence of this quiet time after the holidays.

In the peaceful moments before the new growth of the spring,
Let us pause briefly, breathe deeply, and enjoy the rush of air,
We give our thanks for another year of life, love and prosperity
With confidence that we have planned well for the coming year.

And so it is blessed, favorable, fruitful and fortunate,
Goddess Fortuna!

Blessed be.

A Birthday Prayer

As babes we come into the world, we are healthy, whole and perfect,
Mother and father rejoice at this precious and brief moment in time
And share the good news within our close circle of family and friends.

The babe grows and becomes a child, learning the lessons of family
Within a slowly growing spiral which expands from mother and father
To include extended family, friends, neighbors, the postman and pets.

And then is the moment when the child is schooled at home or away,
And knowledge arrives with independent, yet supervised new friends
And we have faith in the community in which we live, work and learn.

Finally is the time when the child is grown to adulthood, ready to marry
And begin the cycle of life anew; we see parents become grandparents
And the family becomes a branching tree of ancestry and generations.

Today, we honor our birthday, no matter what our age, or place in life,
The miracle of safe and healthy birth which was the first starting point
That provided the sound foundation for our life, choice and free will.

And so it is blessed, favorable, fruitful and fortunate,
Goddess Fortuna Primigenia!

Blessed be.

Annual Prayer for World Peace

As we complete another year of international study
We look back on how much we have learned.
We honor our history, and the history of our friends
As we continue to aspire toward world peace.

And so it is blessed, favorable, fruitful and fortunate,
Goddess Fortuna!

Blessed be.

QUOD BONUM FAUSTUM FELIX FORTUNATUMQUE SIT

Section 102 (Book 1)
from *De Divinatione*
by Marcus Tullius Cicero

Conclusion

The story behind this little book is a personal one; a story which, at first glance, seems very unrelated to the book itself. This book is about a small dog and his owner. In 2007, which seems a very long time ago, miscommunication in my neighborhood resulted in a wall being torn down between properties; an activity which ultimately resulted in the loss of my dog. Despite my efforts to find and return the dog, he has been missing, and the most inspiring idea I have heard is that he was so "cute" that perhaps someone stole him and, hopefully, gave him a nice home.

I have also heard some not-so-nice ideas about what may have happened. Those types of remarks, dear reader, will not be repeated within this book. In the absence of knowing what actually transpired, my imagination was running wild. By 2009 I needed a creative outlet, one which served to keep up my faith that my lost dog was okay. By day, my energies were on career. Afterhours, I was networking, searching the internet, and looking for stories about dogs who returned home after years of wandering. Suddenly, I remembered my dog's birthday.

He was born on June 24, 2003. Not a very remarkable date, considering his half-brother was born on October 31; a fabulous date for dogs who, at least on my household, loved watching the neighborhood kids dress up for a party and drop by for treats. When I searched for his holiday, our choice was between St. John's Day and the Day of the ancient Roman Goddess Fors Fortuna, a pleasant Goddess of good luck or good fortune for ancient Romans. At the time, the ancient Goddess seemed quite glamorous, attractive and fitting for a cute, little, fluffy sort of dog.

Fast forward to 2009, I started taking a closer look at that birth date, and soon thereafter I began to wonder about the people who believed in this Goddess so long ago. It was then that I made a decision to put those worried energies of mine to online research. I discovered that June 24 was one of many dates throughout the year that the Goddess Fortuna was observed in the ancient Roman calendar. Many other aspects of this Goddess were honored in other ways, on other days, throughout the Roman Empire. before very long, this little project started to become huge.

Each holiday of Fortuna had a story; a famous person who built and dedicated a temple for a particular reason or purpose. As I read into these stories, I found insight and morals, sort of like little bible stories …. except these were stories that didn't appear in the bible, because they were distinctly Roman stories and Roman values. As each story wound its tale, I began to wonder if this was, in fact, a spiritual calling. And, if so, should I share these stories as a tribute?

I began to podcast each of the stories, creating a new mock-worship service every week. The show aired live on Sunday morning internet radio, with the idea that there were valuable lessons and tales … amazing stories of women who banded together to stop a war when powerful men had tried and failed, an oracle that rivaled the popularity of the oracle of Delphi for at least a thousand years, insight into Roman marriage, and an eye-opening account of the vast influence of the Goddess Fortuna throughout the Roman Empire into Britain and beyond.

The podcasts expanded to include astrology, NeoPaganism and more Roman Goddess holidays. I started putting together a website. Podcasts were uploaded, calendars were added, and graphics were selected. All this was, at first, to relieve some of my personal pressures; yet the stories themselves began to convince others in ways that have attracted attention from people within a wide range of new age and alternative spiritualities, including NeoPagan, Wiccan, Goddess Spirituality, Roman Reconstructionist, Hellenistic Reconstructionist, and many others.

Musicians, spiritual leaders, icons within alternative spirituality, and just regular people with something to share began to join me in the podcasts. The story-telling began to stretch beyond my personal issues, and my own fascination with the current applicability of lessons learned from ancient spirituality, to a Sunday morning variety package of music, mentors and mantras. In the beginning, I worked with prayers from Mark Ventimiglia's excellent *Pagan Prayer Book.* As time went on, I began writing my own prayers, specifically for aspects of the Goddess Fortuna.

From what appeared to be a very insignificant birth date of a lost dog, a beloved pet that I wished and prayed would return safely home during his lifetime, has become a wealth of knowledge, spirituality and appreciation of ancient tales of ethics and success. This labor of love has brought me strength, love, and unexpected friendships. It has been my pleasure sharing all my praises and supplications for the Goddess Fortuna with you, and if I had three wishes, one would be that reading this book has given you as much pleasure as it has given me to write it.

Brightest Blessings!

www.ingramcontent.com/pod-product-compliance
Lightning Source LLC
LaVergne TN
LVHW031339150826
845673LV00012B/2977

* 9 7 8 1 5 4 6 5 6 1 4 3 9 *